In memory of my mother, Rose Miyako Takahashi Wenjen, who accepted my father's marriage proposal after opening a fortune cookie on their dinner date that encouraged her to take the leap.
—Mia

For Justy and Keiah.
—Colleen

Fortune Cookies for Everyone! The Surprising Story of the Tasty Treat We Love to Eat
Text copyright © 2025 Mia Wenjen
Illustrations copyright © 2025 Colleen Kong-Savage
Published in 2025 by Red Comet Press, LLC, Brooklyn, NY

Smithsonian Asian Pacific American Center:
Mia Cai Cariello, Education Specialist
Andrea Kim Neighbors, Director of Education
Dr. Yao-Fen You, Acting Director

Smithsonian Enterprises:
Avery Naughton, Licensing Coordinator
Paige Towler, Editorial Lead
Jill Corcoran, Senior Director, Licensed Publishing
Brigid Ferraro, Vice President of New Business and Licensing
Carol LeBlanc, President

The Smithsonian name and logo are owned by the Smithsonian Institution and is registered in the U.S. Patent and Trademark Office.

All rights reserved. No part of this book may be used or reproduced in any manner whatsoever without written permission except in the case of brief quotations embodied in critical articles and reviews.

Library of Congress Control Number: 2024948535
ISBN (HB): 978-1-63655-159-3
ISBN (EBOOK): 978-1-63655-160-9

25 26 27 28 29 TLF 10 9 8 7 6 5 4 3 2 1

First Edition
Manufactured in China using FSC paper
Red Comet Press is distributed by ABRAMS, New York
RedCometPress.com

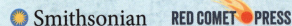

Mia Wenjen   Colleen Kong-Savage

The surprising story of
the tasty treat we love to eat

RED COMET PRESS • BROOKLYN

"The Chinese food is here!" Grandma Miyako called her grandchildren, Kenji and Keiko, down to dinner. "I ordered your favorites! Salt and pepper squid, garlic pea pods, and beef lo mein!"

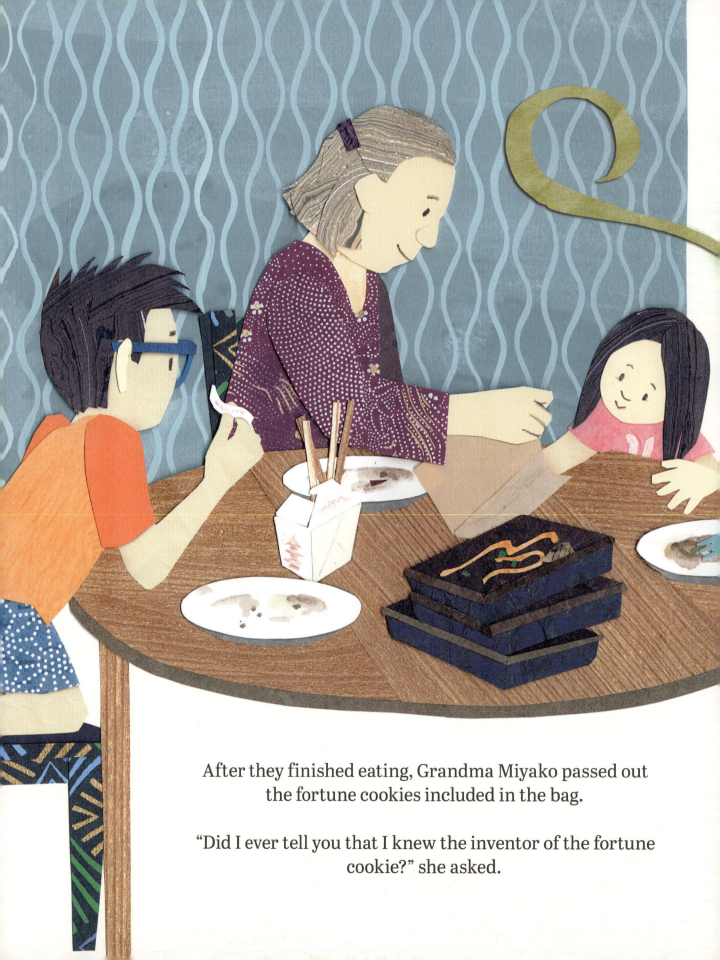

After they finished eating, Grandma Miyako passed out the fortune cookies included in the bag.

"Did I ever tell you that I knew the inventor of the fortune cookie?" she asked.

"You know everyone, Grandma! Tell us more!" her grandchildren begged.

"It is a long and twisty story," she replied with a smile, "not unlike the fortune cookie itself. Let me get my scrapbook."

"Do you know why I take you to Golden Gate Park for tea and fortune cookies? When I was a girl, a man named Makoto Hagiwara ran the Japanese Tea Garden and decided to serve fortune cookies with the tea. He made them by hand using an iron mold called a kata with his initials M.H. on it."

"The fortune cookies were so popular, he needed help. He asked Suyeichi Okamura, my best friend Yukiko's father, to help him, because he ran a bakery. Yukiko's father suggested changing the flavor from salty miso to sweet vanilla and butter to make them more appealing to Americans. It worked!"

"We like the fortune cookies at the Japanese Tea Garden the way they are now," her grandchildren agreed.

"Yukiko's family bakery sold out of fortune cookies every day. Did you know a lot of Japanese Americans in San Francisco ran Chinese restaurants because sushi wasn't popular then? They would include the cookies when they presented the check at the end of the meal."

"For my birthday, Yukiko had a surprise for me at her family's bakery. We tiptoed down to the bakery's basement. Yukiko proudly showed me her father's new machine. The workers removed the hot cookies and wrapped them around a fortune. We ate cookie after cookie. It was a happy day!"

"Everything changed after the Imperial Japanese Navy bombed Pearl Harbor and America entered World War II. We had to pack up only what we could carry and move to a concentration camp."

It made Keiko sad to think about her grandmother being sent away. "Why did you have to go to a concentration camp?" Keiko asked.

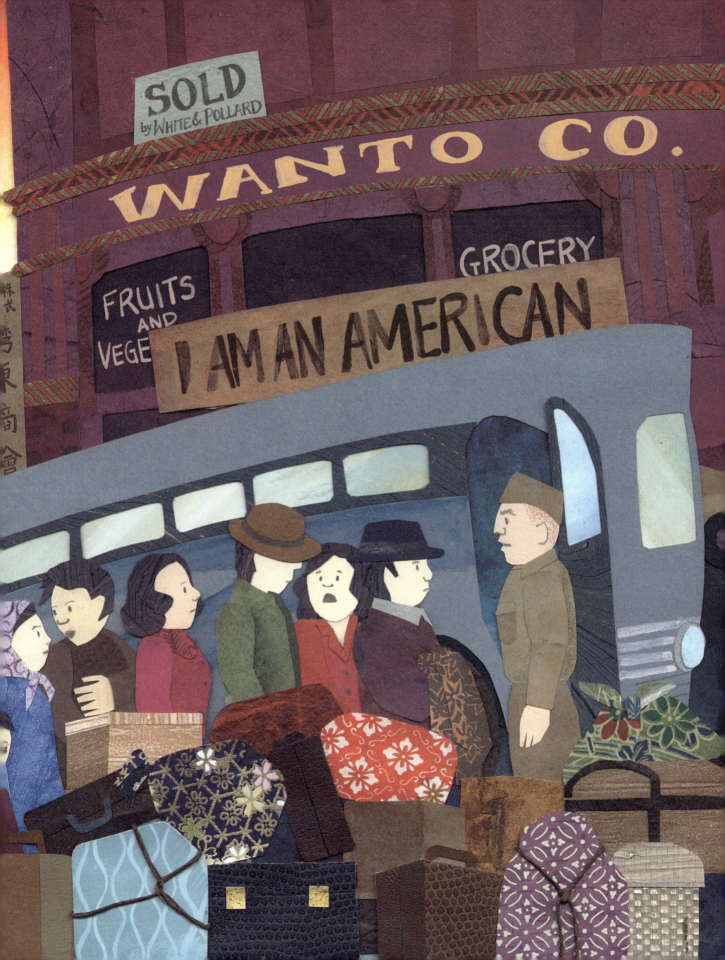

"After the war ended, Yukiko and her family returned home to San Francisco. Their bakery equipment was gone! It was years before her father was able to make fortune cookies again."

"So what happened to the fortune cookies during the war?" Kenji asked.

"During the war, Chinese Americans took over from the Japanese Americans and the fortune cookie got even more popular.

"Before returning home, soldiers often stopped in San Francisco and Los Angeles where they encountered Chinese food and fortune cookies. The soldiers expected fortune cookies at all Chinese restaurants, and they soon became popular across the country."

"In 1983, a mock trial was held where both Los Angeles and San Francisco claimed that the fortune cookie was invented in their city.

"When the Los Angeles bakery, Fugetsu-Do, pulled out their kata as proof, everyone gasped. The molds had the initials M.H. on them! They were Makoto Hagiwara's kata!"

"His kata traveled all the way from San Francisco to Los Angeles!" Kenji exclaimed. "Maybe their kata was the one missing from Yukiko's family's warehouse!"

"My birthday surprise was part of this American invention. And on top of that, San Francisco won!"

"Where do you think the fortune cookie came from?"
Keiko asked.

"As a child, I visited Kyoto's shrines and temples and bought fortunes called omikuji. The streets were filled with shops full of wonderful things to buy, including snacks. My favorite is tsujiura senbei (fortune crackers), a type of Japanese cookie flavored with miso and sesame and folded around a paper fortune."

"Miso was the original flavor of the fortune cookie," Kenji remembered.

"So for me, tsujiura senbei most closely resembles the fortune cookie," she replied.

"Are fortune cookies actually lucky?" wondered Keiko.

"Well, some people have won the lottery with the numbers on the fortune. But more importantly, your grandfather proposed to me at dinner in Chinatown, and the fortune cookie told me to marry him! And now, many years later, we have both of you!"

AUTHOR'S NOTE

I grew up in Southern California eating at Chinese restaurants in Los Angeles's Chinatown. My father emigrated from China to attend UCLA for his PhD in mathematics. He missed authentic Chinese food, so we made a monthly pilgrimage to Chinatown in Los Angeles to stock up on Asian groceries and feast on Chinese food.

My Japanese American mother was born in San Francisco and roller-skated the steep hills of Japantown. She was finishing high school when World War II forced her and family from their home.

I was visiting a bread store in San Francisco's Fisherman's Wharf where I saw a display inside that said the fortune cookie was invented in San Francisco. That seemed reasonable to me. There is both a thriving Chinatown and a bustling Japantown.

But when I tried to look up who invented the fortune cookie, all bets were off. No one seemed to know. I like my food with a side of history, so I dug right in. The mystery of the fortune cookie contains US history—the good, the bad, and the ugly— in a single bite. But most of all, it celebrates immigrants and their pursuit of the American dream.

—Mia

ILLUSTRATOR'S NOTE

I incorporated Japanese design motifs into the illustrations to bring an additional layer of meaning to the art.

The geometric pattern on the scrapbook is Kikko, which represents the shape and pattern of a tortoise shell—symbolizing longevity and strength.

The wallpaper pattern is Tatewaku, which represents undulating steam rising. It can suggest spirits rising or the ability to rise above challenges.

—Colleen

KEY WORDS

Golden Gate Park: a 1,017-acre park located in San Francisco.

Japanese Concentration Camp: President Franklin D. Roosevelt signed Executive Order 9066 on February 19, 1942 forcing people of Japanese ancestry in the US into ten camps predominantly in western America for up to three years.

Kata (kah-tah): small round iron pans used to make fortune cookies by hand.

Makoto Hagiwara (August 15, 1854–September 12, 1925): a Japanese-born American landscape designer who managed the Japanese Tea Garden at Golden Gate Park and is credited for creating the fortune cookie.

Miso: a thick, salty, fermented soybean paste used in Japanese cooking.

Omikuji (oh-me-koo-gee): fortune-telling papers sold at shrines and temples in Japan.

Omikuji senbei (oh-me-ku-gee sen-bay): an alternate name for Japanese fortune crackers.

Senbei (sen bay): a Japanese cookie that can be sweet or savory.

Tsujiura senbei (tsu-gee-ra sen-bay): a type of Japanese fortune cracker.

Mia Wenjen

blogs about parenting, children's books, and education at pragmaticmom.com. She is the co-creator of Multicultural Children's Book Day/Read Your World. She is the author of several illustrated children's books, including *We Sing from the Heart* and *The Traveling Taco*, also from Red Comet Press. Mia lives in Boston with her husband and three kids. Follow her at #PragmaticMom on X, Instagram, Pinterest, and Facebook.

Colleen Kong-Savage

is an Asian American graphic artist and illustrator who also creates murals. She has illustrated two picture books, including *Piano Wants to Play*, which she also wrote. Having lived in places across the globe such as Japan, Malaysia, Philippines, and Zambia, Colleen now makes her home in Queens, New York.